TO

_____

FROM

_____

DATE

_____

Promises from God for Women

© 2015 Christian Art Gifts, RSA
          Christian Art Gifts Inc., IL, USA

First edition 2018

First edition © 2018 Christian Art Publishers
PO Box 1599, Vereeniging, 1930, RSA

Designed by Christian Art Publishers

Images used under license from Shutterstock.com

Printed in China

ISBN 978-1-4321-2719-0

Promises
FROM GOD
FOR WOMEN

CHRISTIAN ART
PUBLISHERS

CONTENTS

IN GOD WE FREELY RECEIVE ...

- ASSURANCE OF SALVATION 7
- BLESSINGS 10
- COMFORT 13
- ENCOURAGEMENT 16
- FAITHFULNESS 19
- FORGIVENESS 22
- GUIDANCE 25
- HOPE 28
- JOY 31
- LOVE 34
- REST AND PEACE OF MIND 37
- SECURITY 40
- STRENGTH 43
- WISDOM 46

HEARTFELT PROMISES IN TIMES OF ...

- ANXIETY.....................................49
- CHANGE.....................................52
- CONFLICT...................................55
- DIFFICULTY.................................58
- DISAPPOINTMENT.......................61
- DOUBT.......................................64
- FAILURE.....................................67
- ILLNESS.....................................70
- LONELINESS...............................73
- SORROW....................................76
- TEMPTATION...............................79

WHAT THE BIBLE SAYS ABOUT ...

- FAITH..82
- FAMILY.......................................85
- FINANCES..................................88
- FRIENDSHIP................................91
- GENTLENESS..............................94
- GOD'S WORD...............................97
- GRACE......................................100
- GRATITUDE................................103
- INNER BEAUTY...........................106
- PRAYER....................................109
- PURPOSE AND POTENTIAL...........112
- SUCCESS..................................115
- TRUTH......................................118
- WORK.......................................121
- WORSHIP...................................124

IN GOD WE
FREELY RECEIVE ...

ASSURANCE OF SALVATION

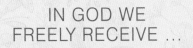

God gave us eternal life,
and this life is in His Son.
Whoever has the Son has life.
1 JOHN 5:11-12 ESV

Our God is a God of salvation.
PSALM 68:20 ESV

Believe in the Lord Jesus,
and you will be saved.
ACTS 16:31 NIV

Everyone who calls on the name
of the Lord will be saved.
ROMANS 10:13 NIV

The LORD takes pleasure
in His people; He adorns
the humble with salvation.
PSALM 149:4 NKJV

Christ died once for all time as
a sacrifice to take away the sins
of many people. He will come
again, not to deal with our sins,
but to bring salvation to all who
are eagerly waiting for Him.

HEBREWS 9:28 NLT

It is the power of God that brings
salvation to everyone who believes.

ROMANS 1:16 NIV

The LORD is my light and my
salvation – whom shall I fear?
The LORD is the stronghold of my
life – of whom shall I be afraid?

PSALM 27:1 NIV

The LORD is the strength of His
people, a fortress of salvation for
His anointed one. Save Your people and
bless Your inheritance; be their Shepherd
and carry them forever.

PSALM 28:8-9 NIV

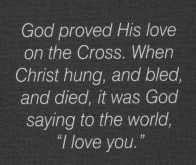

*God proved His love
on the Cross. When
Christ hung, and bled,
and died, it was God
saying to the world,
"I love you."*

Billy Graham

IN GOD WE FREELY RECEIVE ...

BLESSINGS

The blessing of the LORD
makes one rich, and He
adds no sorrow with it.
PROVERBS 10:22 NKJV

The LORD bless you and keep you;
the LORD make His face shine
upon you and be gracious to you;
the LORD lift up His countenance
upon you and give you peace.
NUMBERS 6:24-26 NKJV

Blessed is the one who
trusts in the LORD, whose
confidence is in Him.
JEREMIAH 17:7 NIV

From His abundance we
have all received one gracious
blessing after another.
JOHN 1:16 NLT

BLESSINGS

Blessings crown the
head of the righteous.
PROVERBS 10:6 NIV

The LORD will open the
heavens, the storehouse of His
bounty, to send rain on your
land in season and to bless
all the work of your hands.
DEUTERONOMY 28:12 NIV

The LORD blesses the
dwelling of the righteous.
PROVERBS 3:33 ESV

Praise be to the God and
Father of our Lord Jesus
Christ, who has blessed us in
the heavenly realms with every
spiritual blessing in Christ.
EPHESIANS 1:3 NIV

"Blessed are those who have not
seen and yet have believed."
JOHN 20:29 NIV

Blessed is everyone who fears
the LORD, who walks in His ways!
PSALM 128:1 ESV

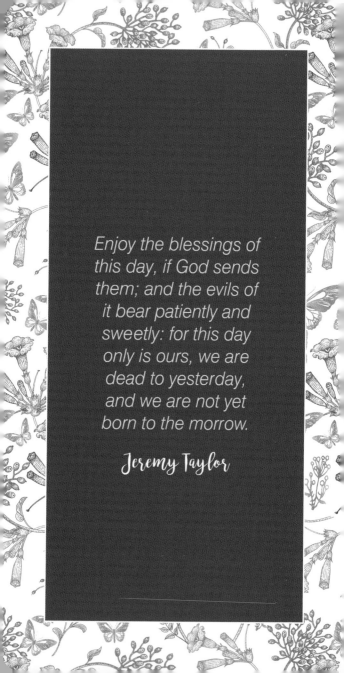

Enjoy the blessings of this day, if God sends them; and the evils of it bear patiently and sweetly: for this day only is ours, we are dead to yesterday, and we are not yet born to the morrow.

Jeremy Taylor

COMFORT

The LORD comforts His
people and will have compassion
on His afflicted ones.
ISAIAH 49:13 NIV

"As a mother comforts her
child, so will I comfort you."
ISAIAH 66:13 NIV

He heals the brokenhearted
and binds up their wounds.
PSALM 147:3 NKJV

Cast your cares on the LORD
and He will sustain you.
PSALM 55:22 NIV

The LORD upholds all
who are falling and raises up
all who are bowed down.
PSALM 145:14 ESV

May Your unfailing love be
my comfort, according to Your
promise to Your servant.
PSALM 119:76 NIV

God will shower us with His
comfort through Christ.
2 CORINTHIANS 1:5 NLT

"I, yes I, am the one who comforts
you. So why are you afraid?"
ISAIAH 51:12 NLT

Praise be to the God and
Father of our Lord Jesus Christ,
the Father of compassion and
the God of all comfort, who
comforts us in all our troubles,
so that we can comfort those in
any trouble with the comfort we
ourselves receive from God.
2 CORINTHIANS 1:3-4 NIV

How great is the goodness You
have stored up for those who fear
You. You lavish it on those who
come to You for protection,
blessing them before the watching world.
PSALM 31:19 NLT

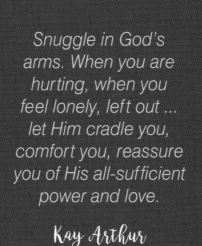

Snuggle in God's arms. When you are hurting, when you feel lonely, left out ... let Him cradle you, comfort you, reassure you of His all-sufficient power and love.

Kay Arthur

ENCOURAGEMENT

May our Lord Jesus Christ
Himself and God our Father,
who loved us and by His grace
gave us eternal encouragement
and good hope, encourage your
hearts and strengthen you in
every good deed and word.

2 THESSALONIANS 2:16-17 NIV

"Be strong and courageous! Do
not be afraid or discouraged.
For the LORD your God is
with you wherever you go."

JOSHUA 1:9 NLT

Worry weighs a person
down; an encouraging
word cheers a person up.

PROVERBS 12:25 NLT

Be strong and courageous;
do not be afraid or lose heart!

1 CHRONICLES 22:13 NLT

ENCOURAGEMENT

Because God wanted to make
the unchanging nature of His
purpose very clear, He confirmed
it with an oath. God did this so
that we may be greatly encouraged.
HEBREWS 6:17-18 NIV

Be of good courage, and He
shall strengthen your heart,
all you who hope in the LORD.
PSALM 31:24 NKJV

"Be encouraged, My child!
Your sins are forgiven."
MATTHEW 9:2 NLT

The Scriptures give us hope and
encouragement as we wait patiently
for God's promises to be fulfilled.
May God, who gives this patience
and encouragement, help you live in
complete harmony with each other.
ROMANS 15:4-5 NLT

God has not given us a spirit
of fear, but of power and of
love and of a sound mind.
2 TIMOTHY 1:7 NKJV

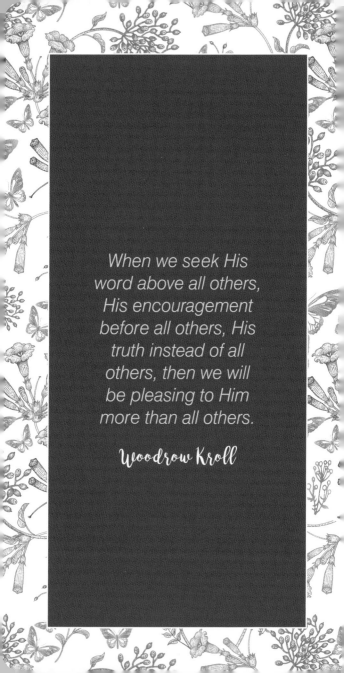

When we seek His word above all others, His encouragement before all others, His truth instead of all others, then we will be pleasing to Him more than all others.

Woodrow Kroll

FAITHFULNESS

Let us hold fast the confession
of our hope without wavering,
for He who promised is faithful.
HEBREWS 10:23 NKJV

Know that the LORD your God, He
is God, the faithful God who keeps
covenant and mercy for a thousand
generations with those who love
Him and keep His commandments.
DEUTERONOMY 7:9 NKJV

The faithful love of the LORD
never ends! His mercies never cease.
Great is His faithfulness; His mercies
begin afresh each morning.
LAMENTATIONS 3:22-23 NLT

The Lord is faithful. He will establish
you and guard you against the evil one.
2 THESSALONIANS 3:3 ESV

The LORD is good; His steadfast
love endures forever, and His
faithfulness to all generations.
PSALM 100:5 ESV

FAITHFULNESS

The LORD is righteous in all His
ways and faithful in all He does.
PSALM 145:17 NIV

He will keep you strong to the
end so that you will be free from
all blame on the day when our
Lord Jesus Christ returns. God will
do this, for He is faithful to do
what He says, and He has invited
you into partnership with His
Son, Jesus Christ our Lord.
1 CORINTHIANS 1:8-9 NLT

Your unfailing love,
O LORD, is as vast as the
heavens; Your faithfulness
reaches beyond the clouds.
PSALM 36:5 NLT

"Heaven and earth will pass
away, but My words will
by no means pass away."
MATTHEW 24:35 NKJV

If we are unfaithful,
He remains faithful, for He
cannot deny who He is.
2 TIMOTHY 2:13 NLT

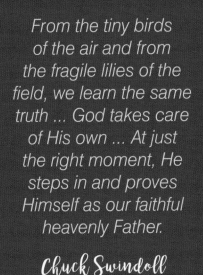

*From the tiny birds
of the air and from
the fragile lilies of the
field, we learn the same
truth ... God takes care
of His own ... At just
the right moment, He
steps in and proves
Himself as our faithful
heavenly Father.*

Chuck Swindoll

FORGIVENESS

The Lord our God is
merciful and forgiving.
DANIEL 9:9 NLT

He is faithful and just and
will forgive us our sins.
1 JOHN 1:9 NIV

As far as the east is from the
west, so far has He removed
our transgressions from us.
PSALM 103:12 NIV

"I will forgive their wickedness,
and I will never again remember
their sins," says the LORD.
HEBREWS 8:12 NLT

If you forgive other people when
they sin against you, your heavenly Father
will also forgive you.
MATTHEW 6:14 NIV

FORGIVENESS

"Though your sins are like
scarlet, they shall be as white
as snow; though they are red as
crimson, they shall be like wool."
ISAIAH 1:18 NIV

"There is forgiveness of
sins for all who repent."
LUKE 24:47 NLT

"This is My blood of the covenant,
which is poured out for many
for the forgiveness of sins."
MATTHEW 26:28 NIV

"Forgive, and you will be forgiven."
LUKE 6:37 ESV

"If you forgive anyone's sins, their
sins are forgiven; if you do not
forgive them, they are not forgiven."
JOHN 20:23 NIV

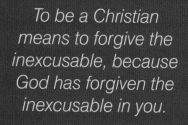

To be a Christian means to forgive the inexcusable, because God has forgiven the inexcusable in you.

C. S. Lewis

GUIDANCE

The LORD says, "I will guide
you along the best pathway
for your life. I will advise
you and watch over you."

PSALM 32:8 NLT

Put your hope in the LORD.
Travel steadily along His path.

PSALM 37:34 NLT

Show me the right path, O LORD;
point out the road for me to follow. Lead
me by Your truth and teach me, for You are
the God who saves me.

PSALM 25:4-5 NLT

May He give you the desire
of your heart and make
all your plans succeed.

PSALM 20:4 NIV

The LORD will guide you always.

ISAIAH 58:11 NIV

God is our God for ever and ever;
He will be our guide even to the end.
PSALM 48:14 NIV

The LORD is good and does
what is right; He shows the proper
path to those who go astray.
PSALM 25:8 NLT

For the word of the LORD
is upright, and all His work
is done in faithfulness.
PSALM 33:4 ESV

Whether you turn to the right
or to the left, your ears will
hear a voice behind you, saying,
"This is the way; walk in it."
ISAIAH 30:21 NIV

The LORD replied, "My Presence will go
with you, and I will give you rest."
EXODUS 33:14 NIV

*Never be
afraid to trust
an unknown
future to a
known God.*

Corrie ten Boom

HOPE

The LORD is good to those
whose hope is in Him, to
the one who seeks Him.
LAMENTATIONS 3:25 NIV

Those who hope in the LORD
will renew their strength. They
will soar on wings like eagles;
they will run and not grow weary,
they will walk and not be faint.
ISAIAH 40:31 NIV

Having hope will give you
courage. You will be protected
and will rest in safety.
JOB 11:18 NLT

We have this hope as an anchor
for the soul, firm and secure. It
enters the inner sanctuary behind
the curtain, where our forerunner,
Jesus, has entered on our behalf.
HEBREWS 6:19-20 NIV

HOPE

Blessed are those whose hope
is in the LORD their God.

PSALM 146:5 NIV

Hope in the LORD! For with
the LORD there is steadfast
love, and with Him is
plentiful redemption.

PSALM 130:7 ESV

The eye of the LORD is on those
who fear Him, on those who
hope in His steadfast love.

PSALM 33:18 ESV

Hope will not lead to
disappointment. For we
know how dearly God
loves us, because He has
given us the Holy Spirit to
fill our hearts with His love.

ROMANS 5:5 NLT

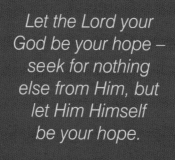

Let the Lord your God be your hope – seek for nothing else from Him, but let Him Himself be your hope.

St. Augustine

Joy

The joy of the LORD is your strength.
NEHEMIAH 8:10 NKJV

"Be happy! Yes, leap for joy! For a great
reward awaits you in heaven."
LUKE 6:23 NLT

Delight yourself in the
LORD and He will give you
the desires of your heart.
PSALM 37:4 ESV

Those who look to Him for help
will be radiant with joy; no shadow
of shame will darken their faces.
PSALM 34:5 NLT

You make known to me the path
of life; in Your presence there is
fullness of joy; at Your right
hand are pleasures forevermore.
PSALM 16:11 ESV

JOY

The precepts of the LORD are
right, giving joy to the heart.
The commands of the LORD are
radiant, giving light to the eyes.
PSALM 19:8 NIV

This is the day that the LORD has made;
let us rejoice and be glad in it.
PSALM 118:24 ESV

I will greatly rejoice in
the LORD, my soul shall be
joyful in my God; for He has
clothed me with the garments of
salvation, He has covered me
with the robe of righteousness.
ISAIAH 61:10 NKJV

"Rejoice because your names
are written in heaven."
LUKE 10:20 NKJV

With joy you will drink deeply
from the fountain of salvation!
ISAIAH 12:3 NLT

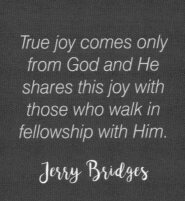

True joy comes only from God and He shares this joy with those who walk in fellowship with Him.

Jerry Bridges

LOVE

For God so loved the world that
He gave His one and only Son,
that whoever believes in Him shall
not perish but have eternal life.
JOHN 3:16 NIV

Give thanks to the LORD, for He is good;
His love endures forever.
PSALM 118:29 NIV

Love is patient, love is kind. It does not
envy, it does not boast, it is not
proud. It is not easily angered, it
keeps no record of wrongs. It always
protects, always trusts, always
hopes, always perseveres.
1 CORINTHIANS 13:4-5, 7 NIV

"Love each other as I have loved you."
JOHN 15:12 NIV

Give thanks to the God of gods.
His love endures forever.
PSALM 136:2 NIV

LOVE

"As the Father has loved Me, so
have I loved you. Abide in My love."
JOHN 15:9 ESV

Nothing in all creation
will ever be able to separate
us from the love of God.
ROMANS 8:39 NLT

"I have loved you with an
everlasting love; I have drawn
you with unfailing kindness."
JEREMIAH 31:3 NIV

"I lavish unfailing love for a
thousand generations on those who love
Me and obey My commands."
DEUTERONOMY 5:10 NLT

This is love: not that we loved God,
but that He loved us and sent His Son
as an atoning sacrifice for our sins.
1 JOHN 4:10 NIV

Though our feelings come and go, God's love for us does not.

C. S. Lewis

IN GOD WE FREELY RECEIVE …

REST AND PEACE OF MIND

My soul finds rest in God;
my salvation comes from Him.

PSALM 62:1 NIV

"Come to Me, all you who
are weary and burdened,
and I will give you rest."

MATTHEW 11:28 NIV

The Sovereign LORD says:
"In repentance and rest is your
salvation, in quietness and
trust is your strength."

ISAIAH 30:15 NIV

Whoever dwells in the shelter
of the Most High will rest in
the shadow of the Almighty.

PSALM 91:1 NIV

The eternal God is your refuge, and His
everlasting arms are under you.

DEUTERONOMY 33:27 NLT

The LORD gives strength to
His people; the LORD blesses
His people with peace.

PSALM 29:11 NIV

"Peace I leave with you; My peace
I give you. Do not let your hearts
be troubled and do not be afraid."

JOHN 14:27 NIV

In peace I will lie down and
sleep, for You alone, LORD,
make me dwell in safety.

PSALM 4:8 NIV

"I will refresh the weary
and satisfy the faint."

JEREMIAH 31:25 NIV

Therefore we do not lose heart.
Though outwardly we are
wasting away, yet inwardly we
are being renewed day by day.

2 CORINTHIANS 4:16 NIV

*If God be our God,
He will give us peace
in trouble: when there
is a storm without,
He will make music
within. The world can
create trouble in peace,
but God can create
peace in trouble.*

Thomas Watson

SECURITY

Your goodness and unfailing
love will pursue me all the days
of my life, and I will live in the
house of the LORD forever.

PSALM 23:6 NLT

"I will put My dwelling place
among you. I will walk
among you and be your God,
and you will be My people."

LEVITICUS 26:11-12 NIV

"Remain in Me, and I will
remain in you. For a branch
cannot produce fruit if it is
severed from the vine, and
you cannot be fruitful
unless you remain in Me."

JOHN 15:4 NLT

"I am with you always,
even to the end of the age."

MATTHEW 28:20 NLT

SECURITY

The LORD is near to all who call on Him, to
all who call on Him in truth.

PSALM 145:18 NIV

Whoever keeps His commandments
abides in God, and God in him.
And by this we know that He abides in us,
by the Spirit whom He has given us.

1 JOHN 3:24 ESV

Let the beloved of the LORD
rest secure in Him, for He
shields him all day long.

DEUTERONOMY 33:12 NIV

The LORD is my rock and my fortress
and my deliverer, my God, my rock, in
whom I take refuge, my shield, and the
horn of my salvation, my stronghold.

PSALM 18:2 ESV

"Though the mountains be shaken
and the hills be removed, yet My
unfailing love for you will not be
shaken nor My covenant of peace
be removed," says the LORD.

ISAIAH 54:10 NIV

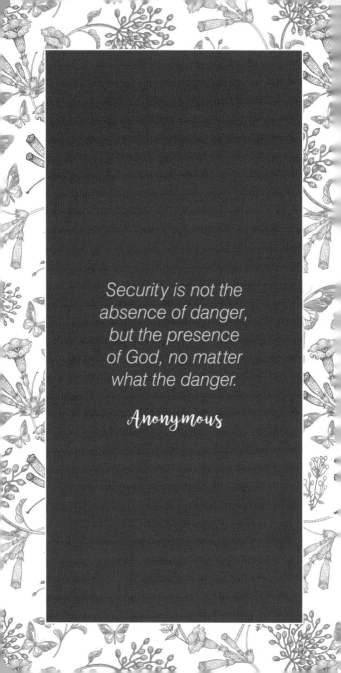

Security is not the absence of danger, but the presence of God, no matter what the danger.

Anonymous

Strength

Be strong in the Lord and
in His mighty power.

EPHESIANS 6:10 NIV

God is my strength and power,
and He makes my way perfect. He
makes my feet like the feet of deer,
and sets me on my high places.

2 SAMUEL 22:33-34 NKJV

God is our refuge and strength,
an ever-present help in trouble.

PSALM 46:1 NIV

The Sovereign Lord is my
strength; He makes my feet like
the feet of a deer, He enables
me to tread on the heights.

HABAKKUK 3:19 NIV

The Lord is my strength and
my song; He has given me victory.

PSALM 118:14 NLT

STRENGTH

I thank and praise You, God
of my ancestors, for You have
given me wisdom and strength.
DANIEL 2:23 NLT

"Do not fear, for I am with
you; do not be dismayed,
for I am your God. I will
strengthen you and help you;
I will uphold you with My
righteous right hand."
ISAIAH 41:10 NIV

In Your strength I can
crush an army; with my
God I can scale any wall.
PSALM 18:29 NLT

"I will seek the lost, and I will
bring back the strayed, and I
will bind up the injured, and
I will strengthen the weak."
EZEKIEL 34:16 ESV

Honor and majesty are
before Him; strength and
gladness are in His place.
1 CHRONICLES 16:27 NKJV

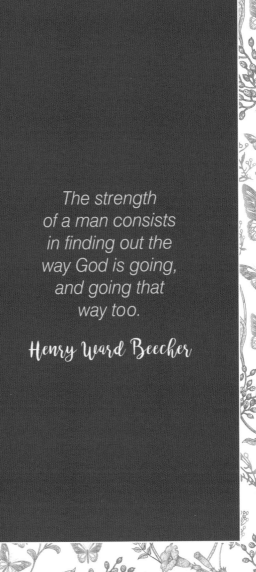

*The strength
of a man consists
in finding out the
way God is going,
and going that
way too.*

Henry Ward Beecher

WISDOM

The wisdom that comes
from heaven is first of all
pure; then peace-loving,
considerate, submissive, full
of mercy and good fruit,
impartial and sincere.

JAMES 3:17 NIV

If you need wisdom, ask
our generous God, and He
will give it to you. He will
not rebuke you for asking.

JAMES 1:5 NLT

Instruct the wise and they
will be wiser still; teach
the righteous and they
will add to their learning.

PROVERBS 9:9 NIV

The law of the LORD is perfect,
refreshing the soul. The statutes
of the LORD are trustworthy,
making wise the simple.

PSALM 19:7 NIV

WISDOM

We know that the Son of God
has come, and He has given us
understanding so that we can
know the true God. And now we
live in fellowship with the true
God because we live in fellowship
with His Son, Jesus Christ.

1 JOHN 5:20 NLT

The LORD gives wisdom;
from His mouth come
knowledge and understanding.

PROVERBS 2:6 NIV

"I will give you the right words
and such wisdom that none
of your opponents will be
able to reply or refute you!"

LUKE 21:15 NLT

God gives wisdom, knowledge,
and joy to those who please Him.

ECCLESIASTES 2:26 NLT

Listen to advice and accept
instruction, that you may
gain wisdom in the future.

PROVERBS 19:20 ESV

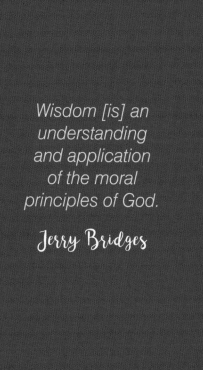

Wisdom [is] an understanding and application of the moral principles of God.

Jerry Bridges

HEARTFELT PROMISES
IN TIMES OF …
ANXIETY

Cast all your anxiety on Him
because He cares for you.
1 PETER 5:7 NIV

Commit everything you do
to the LORD. Trust Him,
and He will help you.
PSALM 37:5 NLT

Do not be afraid or discouraged,
for the LORD will personally
go ahead of you. He will be
with you; He will neither fail
you nor abandon you.
DEUTERONOMY 31:8 NLT

"Be still, and know that I am God."
PSALM 46:10 NKJV

Do not be anxious
about anything, but in
every situation, by prayer and
petition, with thanksgiving,
present your requests to God.
And the peace of God, which
transcends all understanding,
will guard your hearts and
your minds in Christ Jesus.

PHILIPPIANS 4:6-7 NIV

When I thought, "My foot slips,"
Your steadfast love, O LORD, held me up.
When the cares of my heart are many,
Your consolations cheer my soul.

PSALM 94:18-19 ESV

"Therefore I tell you, do not be
anxious about your life, what
you will eat or what you will
drink. Look at the birds of the air:
they neither sow nor reap nor
gather into barns, and yet your
heavenly Father feeds them. Are
you not of more value than they?"

MATTHEW 6:25-26 ESV

Be not miserable about what may happen tomorrow. The same everlasting Father, who cares for you today, will care for you tomorrow.

St. Francis de Sales

CHANGE

There is a time foreverything, and a season
for every activity under the heavens.
ECCLESIASTES 3:1 NIV

Listen, I tell you a mystery:
We will not all sleep, but we
will all be changed – in a
flash, in the twinkling of an
eye, at the last trumpet.
1 CORINTHIANS 15:51-52 NIV

The LORD keeps you from
all harm and watches over
your life. The LORD keeps
watch over you as you come
and go, both now and forever.
PSALM 121:7-8 NLT

LORD, You remain the same
forever! Your throne continues
from generation to generation.
LAMENTATIONS 5:19 NLT

CHANGE

Anyone who belongs to
Christ has become a new
person. The old life is gone;
a new life has begun!
2 CORINTHIANS 5:17 NLT

"I am the LORD,
I do not change; therefore
you are not consumed."
MALACHI 3:6 NKJV

Jesus Christ is the same
yesterday and today and forever.
HEBREWS 13:8 NIV

"You, Lord, laid the
foundation of the earth
in the beginning, and the
heavens are the work of
Your hands; they will
perish, but You remain …
You are the same, and Your
years will have no end."
HEBREWS 1:10-12 ESV

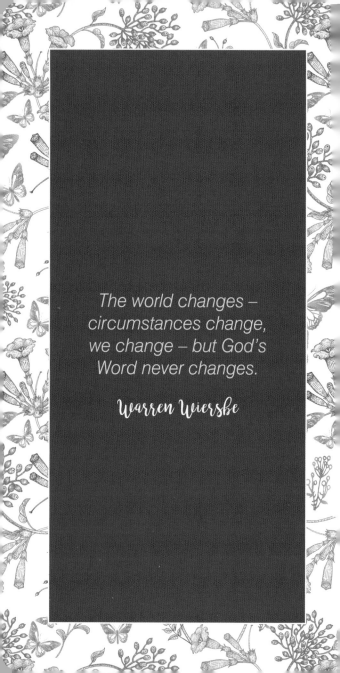

The world changes –
circumstances change,
we change – but God's
Word never changes.

Warren Wiersbe

Conflict

A gentle answer turns away wrath,
but a harsh word stirs up anger.

PROVERBS 15:1 NIV

Bear with each other and
forgive one another if any of you
has a grievance against someone.
Forgive as the Lord forgave you.

COLOSSIANS 3:13 NIV

"In your anger do not sin":
Do not let the sun go down
while you are still angry, and
do not give the devil a foothold.

EPHESIANS 4:26-27 NIV

"Blessed are the peacemakers, for
they will be called children of God."

MATTHEW 5:9 NIV

"First remove the plank from
your own eye, and then you will
see clearly to remove the speck
from your brother's eye."

MATTHEW 7:5 NKJV

CONFLICT

"But I say to you who hear:
Love your enemies, do good to
those who hate you, bless those
who curse you, and pray for
those who spitefully use you."
LUKE 6:27-28 NKJV

You must all be quick
to listen, slow to speak,
and slow to get angry.
JAMES 1:19 NLT

The beginning of strife is
like letting out water, so quit
before the quarrel breaks out.
PROVERBS 17:14 ESV

Never pay back evil with more
evil. Do things in such a way
that everyone can see you are
honorable. Do all that you can
to live in peace with everyone.
ROMANS 12:17-18 NLT

Do not hasten in your spirit
to be angry, for anger rests
in the bosom of fools.
ECCLESIASTES 7:9 NKJV

*Man must evolve
for all human conflict
a method which
rejects revenge,
aggression and
retaliation. The
foundation of such
a method is love.*

Martin Luther King, Jr.

DIFFICULTY

"I am the LORD your
God who takes hold of your
right hand and says to you,
'Do not fear; I will help you.'"
ISAIAH 41:13 NIV

"In Me you may have peace.
In the world you will have
tribulation; but be of good
cheer, I have overcome the world."
JOHN 16:33 NKJV

When troubles come your way,
consider it an opportunity for
great joy. For you know that
when your faith is tested, your
endurance has a chance to grow.
JAMES 1:2-3 NLT

Blessed is the one
who perseveres under trial
because, having stood the
test, that person will receive
the crown of life.
JAMES 1:12 NIV

DIFFICULTY

Let us throw off everything
that hinders and the sin that
so easily entangles. And let us
run with perseverance the
race marked out for us.
HEBREWS 12:1 NIV

Glory in tribulations,
knowing that tribulation
produces perseverance; and
perseverance, character;
and character, hope.
ROMANS 5:3-4 NKJV

"When you go through deep waters,
I will be with you. When you go
through rivers of difficulty, you
will not drown. When you walk
through the fire of oppression,
you will not be burned up; the
flames will not consume you."
ISAIAH 43:2 NLT

"Don't let your hearts be troubled.
Trust in God, and trust also in Me."
JOHN 14:1 NLT

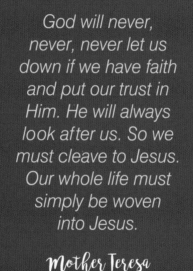

God will never, never, never let us down if we have faith and put our trust in Him. He will always look after us. So we must cleave to Jesus. Our whole life must simply be woven into Jesus.

Mother Teresa

DISAPPOINTMENT

Why are you cast down,
O my soul? And why are you
disquieted within me? Hope in
God, for I shall yet praise Him
for the help of His countenance.

PSALM 42:5 NKJV

The LORD directs the steps of
the godly. He delights in every
detail of their lives. Though they
stumble, they will never fall, for
the LORD holds them by the hand.

PSALM 37:23-24 NLT

"Those who hope in Me
will not be disappointed."

ISAIAH 49:23 NIV

From the fruit of their lips
people are filled with good
things, and the work of their
hands brings them reward.

PROVERBS 12:14 NIV

The LORD is close to the
brokenhearted; He rescues
those whose spirits are crushed.

PSALM 34:18 NLT

For the Scripture says,
"Whoever believes on Him
will not be put to shame."

ROMANS 10:11 NKJV

I am certain that God,
who began the good work
within you, will continue
His work until it is finally
finished on the day when
Christ Jesus returns.

PHILIPPIANS 1:6 NLT

We know that in all things
God works for the good
of those who love Him,
who have been called
according to His purpose.

ROMANS 8:28 NIV

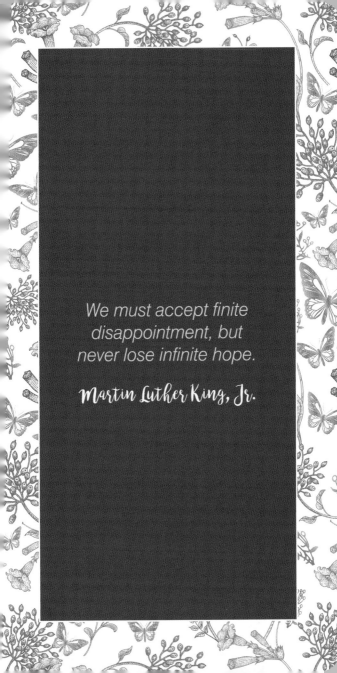

We must accept finite disappointment, but never lose infinite hope.

Martin Luther King, Jr.

DOUBT

When doubts filled my
mind, Your comfort gave
me renewed hope and cheer.
PSALM 94:19 NLT

"Have faith in God. I tell
you the truth, you can say to
this mountain, 'May you be
lifted up and thrown into
the sea,' and it will happen.
But you must really believe
it will happen and have
no doubt in your heart."
MARK 11:22-23 NLT

You must believe and not doubt,
because the one who doubts
is like a wave of the sea, blown
and tossed by the wind.
JAMES 1:6 NIV

Listen! The LORD's arm is not
too weak to save you, nor is His
ear too deaf to hear you call.
ISAIAH 59:1 NLT

DOUBT

"'My purpose will stand,
and I will do all that I please.'
What I have said, that I will
bring about; what I have
planned, that I will do."
ISAIAH 46:10-11 NIV

God's way is perfect. All the
LORD's promises prove true.
He is a shield for all who
look to Him for protection.
PSALM 18:30 NLT

Trust in the LORD with all
your heart, and lean not on
your own understanding; in all
your ways acknowledge Him,
and He shall direct your paths.
PROVERBS 3:5-7 NKJV

The LORD is not slow to
fulfill His promise as some
count slowness, but is patient
toward you, not wishing that
any should perish, but that
all should reach repentance.
2 PETER 3:9 ESV

Nothing is too great and nothing is too small to commit into the hands of the Lord.

A. W. Pink

FAILURE

The godly may trip seven times,
but they will get up again.
But one disaster is enough
to overthrow the wicked.

PROVERBS 24:16 NLT

We are hard-pressed on every
side, yet not crushed; we are
perplexed, but not in despair;
persecuted, but not forsaken;
struck down, but not destroyed.

2 CORINTHIANS 4:8-9 NKJV

He will not let your
foot slip – He who watches
over you will not slumber.
The LORD watches over you –
the LORD is your shade
at your right hand; the sun
will not harm you by day,
nor the moon by night.

PSALM 121:3, 5-6 NIV

He said to me, "My grace
is sufficient for you, for My
power is made perfect in
weakness." Therefore I will
boast all the more gladly of my
weaknesses, so that the power
of Christ may rest upon me.
2 CORINTHIANS 12:9 NIV

Be strong and courageous and
do it. Do not be afraid and do not
be dismayed, for the LORD God,
even my God, is with you. He will
not leave you or forsake you, until
all the work for the service of the
house of the LORD is finished.
1 CHRONICLES 28:20 ESV

God had planned
something better for us.
HEBREWS 11:40 NIV

Look after each other so
that none of you fails to
receive the grace of God.
HEBREWS 12:15 NLT

*Be of good cheer.
Do not think of
today's failures,
but of the success
that may come
tomorrow.*

Helen Keller

Illness

My health may fail, and my
spirit may grow weak, but God
remains the strength of my
heart; He is mine forever.

PSALM 73:26 NLT

"I am the LORD who heals you."

EXODUS 15:26 NLT

Bless the LORD, O my soul,
and forget not all His benefits,
who forgives all your iniquity,
who heals all your diseases.

PSALM 103:2-3 NKJV

O LORD my God, I cried to You for help,
and You restored my health.

PSALM 30:2 NLT

Fear the LORD and turn
away from evil. Then you will
have healing for your body
and strength for your bones.

PROVERBS 3:7-8 NLT

"I will be your God throughout
your lifetime – until your hair
is white with age. I made you,
and I will care for you. I will
carry you along and save you."

ISAIAH 46:4 NLT

As soon as I pray, You
answer me; You encourage
me by giving me strength.

PSALM 138:3 NLT

The LORD is the everlasting
God, the Creator of the ends of
the earth. He does not faint or
grow weary; His understanding
is unsearchable. He gives power
to the faint, and to him who has
no might He increases strength.

ISAIAH 40:28-29 ESV

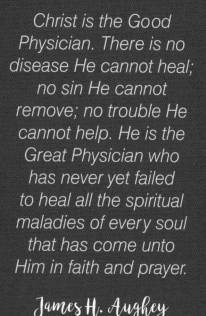

Christ is the Good Physician. There is no disease He cannot heal; no sin He cannot remove; no trouble He cannot help. He is the Great Physician who has never yet failed to heal all the spiritual maladies of every soul that has come unto Him in faith and prayer.

James H. Aughey

LONELINESS

If I go up to the heavens,
You are there; if I make my
bed in the depths, You are
there. If I rise on the wings
of the dawn, if I settle on the
far side of the sea, even there
Your hand will guide me, Your
right hand will hold me fast.

PSALM 139:8-10 NIV

I see that the LORD is always
with me. I will not be shaken,
for He is right beside me.

ACTS 2:25 NLT

"I am with you, and I will
protect you wherever you go.
One day I will bring you back to
this land. I will not leave you
until I have finished giving you
everything I have promised you."

GENESIS 28:15 NLT

"I will never leave you
nor forsake you."

HEBREWS 13:5 NKJV

You shall call, and the LORD
will answer; you shall cry, and
He will say, "Here I am."
ISAIAH 58:9 NKJV

"I will ask the Father, and He
will give you another Advocate,
who will never leave you. He is
the Holy Spirit, who leads into
all truth. He lives with you
now and later will be in you."
JOHN 14:16-17 NLT

The LORD will not forsake
His people, for His great name's
sake, because it has pleased the
LORD to make you His people.
1 SAMUEL 12:22 NKJV

"I will not abandon you as
orphans – I will come to you."
JOHN 14:18 NLT

The LORD will not forsake you.
DEUTERONOMY 4:31 NKJV

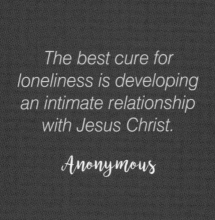

The best cure for loneliness is developing an intimate relationship with Jesus Christ.

Anonymous

Sorrow

"I will rejoice over Jerusalem
and delight in My people. And
the sound of weeping and crying
will be heard in it no more."

ISAIAH 65:19 NLT

"Blessed are those who mourn,
for they will be comforted."

MATTHEW 5:4 NIV

The LORD is good to all; He has
compassion on all He has made.

PSALM 145:9 NIV

"He will wipe every tear
from their eyes, and there
will be no more death or
sorrow or crying or pain."

REVELATION 21:4 NLT

"Truly, truly, I say to you, you will
weep and lament, but the world
will rejoice. You will be sorrowful,
but your sorrow will turn into joy."

JOHN 16:20 ESV

SORROW

Do not grieve like the rest of
mankind, who have no hope.
For we believe that Jesus died
and rose again, and so we
believe that God will bring
with Jesus those who have
fallen asleep in Him.

1 THESSALONIANS 4:13-14 NIV

Weeping may last through the night,
but joy comes with the morning.

PSALM 30:5 NLT

You, God, see the trouble of
the afflicted; You consider their
grief and take it in hand.

PSALM 10:14 NIV

"I will turn their mourning
into gladness; I will give them
comfort and joy instead of sorrow."

JEREMIAH 31:13 NIV

Godly sorrow brings repentance
that leads to salvation and leaves no regret,
but worldly sorrow brings death.

2 CORINTHIANS 7:10 NIV

*How fast we learn
in a day of sorrow!
Scripture shines out in
a new effulgence; every
verse seems to contain
a sunbeam, every
promise stands out in
illuminated splendor.*

Horatius Bonar

TEMPTATION

No temptation has overtaken
you that is not common to man.
God is faithful, and He will not let
you be tempted beyond your ability,
but with the temptation He will
also provide the way of escape,
that you may be able to endure it.

1 CORINTHIANS 10:13 ESV

God blesses those who patiently
endure testing and temptation.
Afterward they will receive the
crown of life that God has
promised to those who love Him.
And remember, when you are
being tempted, do not say, "God
is tempting me." God is never
tempted to do wrong, and He never
tempts anyone else. Temptation
comes from our own desires,
which entice us and drag us away.

JAMES 1:12-14 NLT

TEMPTATION

Because He Himself
suffered when He was
tempted, He is able to help
those who are being tempted.
HEBREWS 2:18 NIV

The Lord knows how to
rescue the godly from trials,
and to keep the unrighteous
under punishment until the day
of judgment, and especially those
who indulge in the lust of defiling
passion and despise authority.
2 PETER 2:9-10 ESV

Put on the whole armor of God,
that you may be able to stand against the
schemes of the devil. For we do not wrestle
against flesh and blood, but against the
rulers, against the authorities, against
the cosmic powers over this present
darkness, against the spiritual forces of evil
in the heavenly places. Therefore take up
the whole armor of God, that you may be
able to withstand in the evil day, and
having done all, to stand firm.
EPHESIANS 6:11-13 ESV

The realization of God's presence is the one sovereign remedy against temptation.

François Fénelon

WHAT THE BIBLE SAYS ABOUT ...

FAITH

Faith is confidence in what
we hope for and assurance
about what we do not see.
HEBREWS 11:1 NIV

Make every effort to supplement
your faith with virtue, and virtue
with knowledge, and knowledge
with self-control, and self-control
with steadfastness, and steadfastness
with godliness, and godliness
with brotherly affection, and
brotherly affection with love.
2 PETER 1:5-7 ESV

Since we have been justified
through faith, we have peace with
God through our Lord Jesus Christ.
ROMANS 5:1 NIV

Be on your guard;
stand firm in the faith;
be courageous; be strong.
1 CORINTHIANS 16:13 NIV

In the gospel the
righteousness of God is revealed –
a righteousness that is by faith from
first to last, just as it is written:
"The righteous will live by faith."
ROMANS 1:17 NIV

Because of Christ and our
faith in Him, we can now come boldly
and confidently into God's presence.
EPHESIANS 3:12 NLT

Whoever believes in the
Son has eternal life.
JOHN 3:36 NIV

"The Son of Man must be lifted
up, that everyone who believes
in Him may have eternal life."
JOHN 3:14-15 ESV

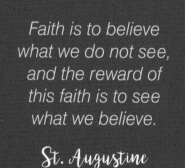

*Faith is to believe
what we do not see,
and the reward of
this faith is to see
what we believe.*

St. Augustine

FAMILY

"All your children will be
taught by the LORD, and
great will be their peace."
ISAIAH 54:13 NIV

Children are a heritage
from the LORD, the fruit
of the womb a reward.
PSALM 127:3 ESV

Direct your children onto the
right path, and when they are
older, they will not leave it.
PROVERBS 22:6 NLT

Do not provoke your children to
anger, but bring them up in the
discipline and instruction of the Lord.
EPHESIANS 6:4 ESV

Her children stand and bless her.
Her husband praises her: "There are
many virtuous and capable women in
the world, but you surpass them all!"
PROVERBS 31:28-29 NLT

FAMILY

The believing wife brings
holiness to her marriage,
and the believing husband
brings holiness to his
marriage. Otherwise, your
children would not be holy,
but now they are holy.
1 CORINTHIANS 7:14 NLT

"Honor your father and
mother. Then you will live a
long, full life in the land the
LORD your God is giving you."
EXODUS 20:12 NLT

As for me and my household,
we will serve the LORD.
JOSHUA 24:15 NIV

Grandchildren are the crowning
glory of the aged; parents are
the pride of their children.
PROVERBS 17:6 NLT

Children, obey your
parents in everything,
for this pleases the Lord.
COLOSSIANS 3:20 NIV

*Each day of
our lives we
make deposits in
the memory banks
of our children.*

Charles Swindoll

FINANCES

"Your Father knows the things you
have need of before you ask Him."
MATTHEW 6:8 NKJV

"Give, and it will be given to you.
A good measure, pressed down,
shaken together and running over,
will be poured into your lap.
For with the measure you use,
it will be measured to you."
LUKE 6:38 NIV

"Bring all the tithes into the
storehouse so there will be
enough food in My Temple.
If you do," says the LORD of
Heaven's Armies, "I will open the
windows of heaven for you. I will
pour out a blessing so great you
won't have enough room to take it
in. Try it! Put Me to the test!"
MALACHI 3:10 NLT

God will supply every need
of yours according to His
riches in glory in Christ Jesus.

PHILIPPIANS 4:19 ESV

"When you give to someone in
need, don't let your left hand
know what your right hand is
doing. Give your gifts in private,
and your Father, who sees
everything, will reward you."

MATTHEW 6:3-4 NLT

"Seek the Kingdom of God
above all else, and live
righteously, and He will give
you everything you need."

MATTHEW 6:33 NLT

*We are not cisterns
made for hoarding,
we are channels
made for sharing.*

Billy Graham

FRIENDSHIP

Two people are better off than
one, for they can help each other
succeed. If one person falls, the
other can reach out and help.
ECCLESIASTES 4:9-10 NLT

As iron sharpens iron,
so a friend sharpens a friend.
PROVERBS 27:17 NLT

Share each other's burdens, and
in this way obey the law of Christ.
GALATIANS 6:2 NLT

Perfume and incense bring
joy to the heart, and the
pleasantness of a friend springs
from their heartfelt advice.
PROVERBS 27:9 NIV

Walk with the wise and
become wise; associate with
fools and get in trouble.
PROVERBS 13:20 NLT

FRIENDSHIP

Don't befriend angry people
or associate with hot-tempered
people, or you will learn to be like
them and endanger your soul.
PROVERBS 22:24-25 NIV

Where there is no guidance,
a people falls, but in an abundance
of counselors there is safety.
PROVERBS 11:14 ESV

There are "friends" who destroy
each other, but a real friend
sticks closer than a brother.
PROVERBS 18:24 NLT

"No longer do I call you servants,
for the servant does not know
what his master is doing; but I
have called you friends, for all
that I have heard from My Father
I have made known to you."
JOHN 15:15 ESV

The friendship of the LORD is
for those who fear Him, and He
makes known to them His covenant.
PSALM 25:14 ESV

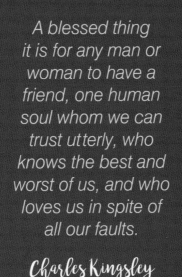

A blessed thing
it is for any man or
woman to have a
friend, one human
soul whom we can
trust utterly, who
knows the best and
worst of us, and who
loves us in spite of
all our faults.

Charles Kingsley

Gentleness

Be completely humble and
gentle; be patient, bearing
with one another in love.
EPHESIANS 4:2 NIV

Let your gentleness be evident
to all. The Lord is near.
PHILIPPIANS 4:5 NIV

Don't repay evil for evil.
Don't retaliate with insults
when people insult you.
Instead, pay them back with
a blessing. That is what God
has called you to do, and He
will grant you His blessing.
1 PETER 3:9 NLT

The meek shall inherit the
land and delight themselves
in abundant peace.
PSALM 37:11 ESV

GENTLENESS

Pursue righteousness and a godly
life, along with faith, love,
perseverance, and gentleness.

1 TIMOTHY 6:11 NLT

"Take My yoke upon you. Let Me
teach you, because I am humble
and gentle at heart, and you
will find rest for your souls."

MATTHEW 11:29 NLT

Therefore, as God's
chosen people, holy
and dearly loved, clothe
yourselves with compassion,
kindness, humility,
gentleness and patience.

COLOSSIANS 3:12 NIV

A servant of the Lord must not
quarrel but be gentle to all, able
to teach, patient, in humility
correcting those who are in
opposition, if God perhaps will
grant them repentance, so
that they may know the truth.

2 TIMOTHY 2:24-25 NKJV

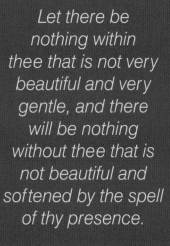

*Let there be
nothing within
thee that is not very
beautiful and very
gentle, and there
will be nothing
without thee that is
not beautiful and
softened by the spell
of thy presence.*

James Allen

God's Word

Everything that was
written in the past was
written to teach us, so
that through the endurance
taught in the Scriptures and
the encouragement they
provide we might have hope.

ROMANS 15:4 NIV

The word of God is alive
and active. Sharper than any
double-edged sword, it penetrates
even to dividing soul and spirit,
joints and marrow; it judges the
thoughts and attitudes of the heart.

HEBREWS 4:12 NIV

In the beginning the Word
already existed. The Word was
with God, and the Word was
God. He existed in the beginning
with God. God created everything
through Him, and nothing was
created except through Him.

JOHN 1:1-3 NLT

GOD'S WORD

Study this Book of Instruction
continually. Meditate on it day
and night so you will be sure to
obey everything written in it.
Only then will you prosper
and succeed in all you do.
JOSHUA 1:8 NLT

Your word is a lamp to guide
my feet and a light for my path.
PSALM 119:105 NLT

"If you remain in Me and My words
remain in you, ask whatever you
wish, and it will be done for you."
JOHN 15:7 NIV

Every word of God proves
true; He is a shield to those
who take refuge in Him.
PROVERBS 30:5 ESV

"Even more blessed are all
who hear the word of God
and put it into practice."
LUKE 11:28 NLT

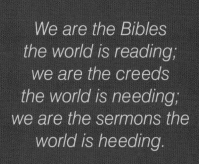

*We are the Bibles
the world is reading;
we are the creeds
the world is needing;
we are the sermons the
world is heeding.*

Billy Graham

GRACE

To each one of us grace
was given according to the
measure of Christ's gift.

EPHESIANS 4:7 NKJV

He gives us grace and glory.
The LORD will withhold
no good thing from those
who do what is right.

PSALM 84:11 NLT

Let us then with confidence draw
near to the throne of grace, that
we may receive mercy and find
grace to help in time of need.

HEBREWS 4:16 ESV

God is able to make all
grace abound to you, so that
having all sufficiency in all
things at all times, you may
abound in every good work.

2 CORINTHIANS 9:8 ESV

God saved us and called us
to live a holy life. He did this,
not because we deserved it,
but because that was His plan
from before the beginning
of time – to show us His
grace through Christ Jesus.
2 TIMOTHY 1:9 NLT

After you have suffered a
little while, the God of all
grace, who has called you to
His eternal glory in Christ,
will Himself restore, confirm,
strengthen, and establish you.
1 PETER 5:10 ESV

In Him we have
redemption through His
blood, the forgiveness
of sins, in accordance with
the riches of God's grace.
EPHESIANS 1:7 NIV

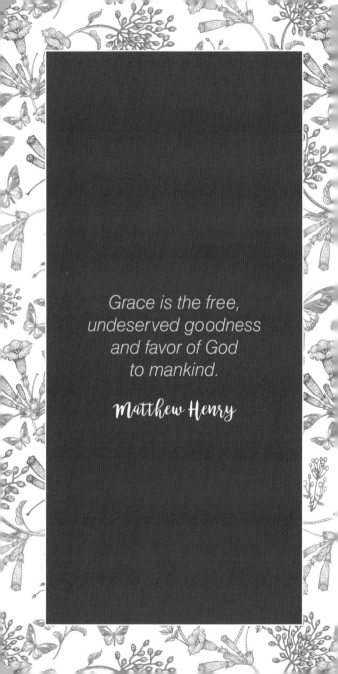

*Grace is the free,
undeserved goodness
and favor of God
to mankind.*

Matthew Henry

GRATITUDE

Give thanks in all
circumstances; for this
is God's will for you
in Christ Jesus.

1 THESSALONIANS 5:18 NIV

Thanks be to God, who always
leads us in Christ's triumphal
procession and uses us to
spread the aroma of the
knowledge of Him everywhere.

2 CORINTHIANS 2:14 NIV

You make me glad
by Your deeds, LORD;
I sing for joy at what
Your hands have done.

PSALM 92:4 NIV

It is good to give thanks
to the LORD, to sing
praises to the Most High.

PSALM 92:1 NLT

GRATITUDE

We thank You, O God! We give
thanks because You are near.
PSALM 75:1 NLT

The LORD has done great things
for us, and we are filled with joy.
PSALM 126:3 NIV

Thanks be to God for
His indescribable gift!
2 CORINTHIANS 9:15 NIV

Give thanks to the LORD,
for He is good! His faithful
love endures forever.
PSALM 107:1 NLT

Thanks be to God! He gives
us the victory through
our Lord Jesus Christ.
1 CORINTHIANS 15:57 NIV

These gates lead to the presence
of the LORD, and the godly enter
there. I thank You for answering
my prayer and giving me victory!
PSALM 118:20-21 NLT

*A state of mind
that sees God in
everything is evidence
of growth in grace and
a thankful heart.*

Charles Finney

Inner beauty

"Blessed are the pure in heart,
for they shall see God."

MATTHEW 5:8 NKJV

Charm is deceptive, and beauty
is fleeting; but a woman who
fears the LORD is to be praised.

PROVERBS 31:30 NIV

"The LORD does not look
at the things people look at.
People look at the outward
appearance, but the LORD
looks at the heart."

1 SAMUEL 16:7 NIV

Your beauty should not come
from outward adornment, such as
elaborate hairstyles and the wearing
of gold jewelry or fine clothes.
Rather, it should be that of your
inner self, the unfading beauty of
a gentle and quiet spirit, which is
of great worth in God's sight.

1 PETER 3:3-4 NIV

INNER BEAUTY

"All those who exalt
themselves will be humbled,
and those who humble
themselves will be exalted."
LUKE 14:11 NIV

You are altogether beautiful, my
darling, beautiful in every way.
SONG OF SOLOMON 4:7 NLT

God is working in you,
giving you the desire and the
power to do what pleases Him.
PHILIPPIANS 2:13 NLT

"Physical training is good, but
training for godliness is much
better, promising benefits in
this life and in the life to come."
1 TIMOTHY 4:8 NLT

I will praise You, for I am
fearfully and wonderfully made;
marvelous are Your works, and
that my soul knows very well.
PSALM 139:14 NKJV

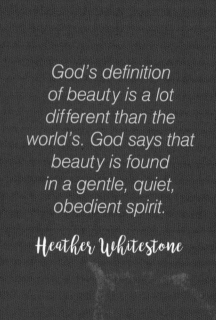

*God's definition
of beauty is a lot
different than the
world's. God says that
beauty is found
in a gentle, quiet,
obedient spirit.*

Heather Whitestone

WHAT THE BIBLE SAYS ABOUT ...
Prayer

The prayer of a righteous person
is powerful and effective.

JAMES 5:16 NIV

"If you believe, you will receive
whatever you ask for in prayer."

MATTHEW 21:22 NIV

"Before they call I will answer;
while they are still speaking I will hear."

ISAIAH 65:24 NIV

The eyes of the Lord are on
the righteous and His ears are
attentive to their prayer.

1 PETER 3:12 NIV

"Ask and it will be given to you;
seek and you will find; knock and
the door will be opened to you."

MATTHEW 7:7 NIV

"You will call on Me and
come and pray to Me,
and I will listen to you."

JEREMIAH 29:12 NIV

PRAYER

Pray in the Spirit on
all occasions with all kinds
of prayers and requests.
With this in mind, be alert
and always keep on praying
for all the Lord's people.
EPHESIANS 6:18 NIV

When you pray, go into
your room, close the door
and pray to your Father,
who is unseen. Then your
Father, who sees what is done
in secret, will reward you.
MATTHEW 6:6 NIV

"If two of you agree here on
earth concerning anything
you ask, My Father in
heaven will do it for you."
MATTHEW 18:19 NLT

Build each other up in your
most holy faith, pray in the
power of the Holy Spirit.
JUDE 20 NLT

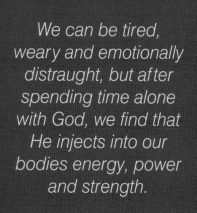

*We can be tired,
weary and emotionally
distraught, but after
spending time alone
with God, we find that
He injects into our
bodies energy, power
and strength.*

Charles Stanley

PURPOSE AND POTENTIAL

You saw me before I was
born. Every day of my life was
recorded in Your book. Every
moment was laid out before
a single day had passed.

PSALM 139:16 NLT

You can make many plans, but
the LORD's purpose will prevail.

PROVERBS 19:21 NLT

"I know the plans I have
for you," declares the LORD,
"plans to prosper you and not
to harm you, plans to give
you hope and a future."

JEREMIAH 29:11 NIV

I cry out to God Most High, to God who
fulfills His purpose for me.

PSALM 57:2 NLT

The counsel of the LORD stands forever,
the plans of His heart to all generations.

PSALM 33:11 NKJV

The world is passing away along
with its desires, but whoever does
the will of God abides forever.

1 JOHN 2:17 ESV

Teach me to do Your will, for
You are my God! Let Your good
Spirit lead me on level ground!

PSALM 143:10 ESV

God has now revealed to us His
mysterious plan regarding Christ,
a plan to fulfill His own good
pleasure. And this is the plan:
At the right time He will bring
everything together under the
authority of Christ – everything
in heaven and on earth.

EPHESIANS 1:9-10 NLT

The LORD has made
everything for its purpose.

PROVERBS 16:4 ESV

*All of God's people
are ordinary people
who have been made
extraordinary by
the purpose He has
given them.*

Oswald Chambers

SUCCESS

Oh, the joys of those who do not
follow the advice of the wicked …
They delight in the law of the LORD,
meditating on it day and night.
They are like trees planted along
the riverbank, bearing fruit each
season. Their leaves never wither,
and they prosper in all they do.

PSALM 1:1-3 NLT

Some trust in chariots and
some in horses, but we trust in
the name of the LORD our God.
They collapse and fall, but
we rise and stand upright.

PSALM 20:7-8 ESV

You will succeed in whatever
you choose to do, and light will
shine on the road ahead of you.

JOB 22:28 NLT

SUCCESS

How joyful are those who fear
the LORD and delight in obeying
His commands. Their children
will be successful everywhere;
an entire generation of godly
people will be blessed. They
themselves will be wealthy, and
their good deeds will last forever.
PSALM 112:1-3 NLT

Commit your work to the LORD,
and your plans will be established.
PROVERBS 16:3 ESV

Do not forget my teaching,
but let your heart keep my
commandments, for length of
days and years of life and peace
they will add to you. So you
will find favor and good success
in the sight of God and man.
PROVERBS 3:1-2, 4 ESV

Remember the LORD your God.
He is the one who gives you
power to be successful.
DEUTERONOMY 8:18 NLT

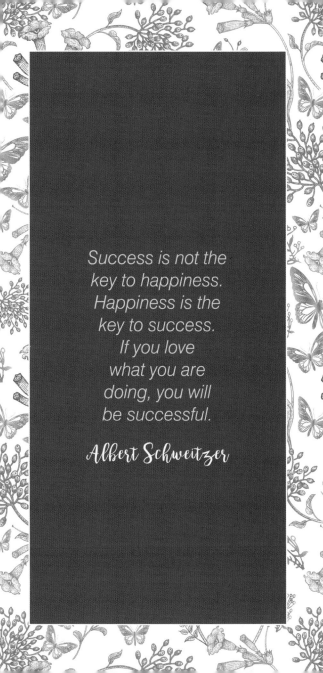

Success is not the
key to happiness.
Happiness is the
key to success.
If you love
what you are
doing, you will
be successful.

Albert Schweitzer

TRUTH

Send out Your light
and Your truth; let them
guide me. Let them lead me
to Your holy mountain, to
the place where You live.

PSALM 43:3 NLT

"You will know the truth,
and the truth will set you free."

JOHN 8:32 NIV

He shall cover you with
His feathers, and under His
wings you shall take refuge;
His truth shall be your shield.

PSALM 91:4 NKJV

Jesus answered, "I am the way
and the truth and the life."

JOHN 14:6 NIV

The truth of the LORD
endures forever.

PSALM 117:2 NKJV

TRUTH

In Him you also trusted, after you
heard the word of truth, the gospel
of your salvation; in whom also,
having believed, you were sealed
with the Holy Spirit of promise, who
is the guarantee of our inheritance
until the redemption of the purchased
possession, to the praise of His glory.

EPHESIANS 1:13-14 NKJV

All Your words are
true; all Your righteous
laws are eternal.

PSALM 119:160 NIV

Every good and perfect gift
is from above, coming down
from the Father of the heavenly
lights, who does not change
like shifting shadows. He chose
to give us birth through the word
of truth, that we might be a kind
of firstfruits of all He created.

JAMES 1:17-18 NIV

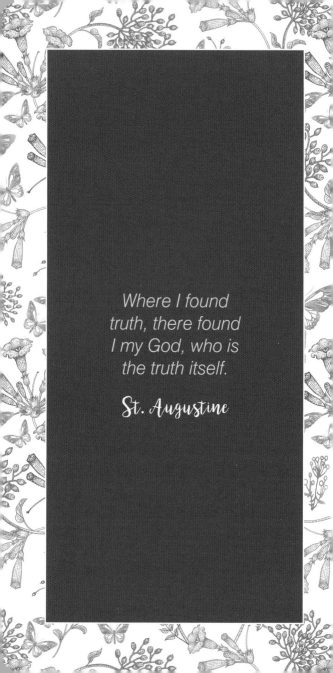

Where I found truth, there found I my God, who is the truth itself.

St. Augustine

WORK

Whatever you do, work
at it with all your heart,
as working for the Lord.
COLOSSIANS 3:23 NIV

The LORD your God will bless
you in all your harvest and in
all the work of your hands,
and your joy will be complete.
DEUTERONOMY 16:15 NIV

A hard worker has plenty
of food, but a person who
chases fantasies has no sense.
PROVERBS 12:11 NLT

You shall eat the fruit of
the labor of your hands; you
shall be blessed, and it
shall be well with you.
PSALM 128:2 ESV

Work brings profit,
but mere talk leads to
poverty! Wealth is a
crown for the wise; the
effort of fools yields
only foolishness.

PROVERBS 14:23-24 NLT

My dear brothers and sisters,
be strong and immovable.
Always work enthusiastically
for the Lord, for you know
that nothing you do for
the Lord is ever useless.

1 CORINTHIANS 15:58 NLT

Let the favor of the LORD
our God be upon us, and
establish the work of our
hands upon us; yes, establish
the work of our hands!

PSALM 90:17 ESV

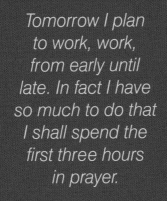

*Tomorrow I plan
to work, work,
from early until
late. In fact I have
so much to do that
I shall spend the
first three hours
in prayer.*

Martin Luther

WORSHIP

Let us worship and bow
down; let us kneel before
the LORD, our Maker!

PSALM 95:6 ESV

"God is Spirit, so those who
worship Him must worship
in spirit and in truth."

JOHN 4:24 NLT

"Where two or three are
gathered together in My name,
I am there in the midst of them."

MATTHEW 18:20 NKJV

Exalt the LORD our God, and
worship at His holy mountain;
for the LORD our God is holy!

PSALM 99:9 ESV

Sing to the LORD, for He
has done excellent things;
this is known in all the earth.

ISAIAH 12:5 NKJV

Give to the LORD the glory due
His name; bring an offering, and
come before Him. Oh, worship the
LORD in the beauty of holiness!

1 CHRONICLES 16:29 NKJV

Since we are receiving a
Kingdom that is unshakable,
let us be thankful and please
God by worshiping Him
with holy fear and awe.

HEBREWS 12:28 NLT

"The hour is coming, and now
is, when the true worshipers
will worship the Father in spirit
and truth; for the Father is
seeking such to worship Him."

JOHN 4:23 NKJV

Sing praises to God and to
His name! Sing loud praises
to Him who rides the clouds.
His name is the Lord –
rejoice in His presence!

PSALM 68:4 NLT

My people, hear my teaching;
listen to the words of my mouth.

PSALM 78:1 NIV

For of Him and through
Him and to Him are all things,
to whom be glory forever. Amen.

ROMANS 11:36 NKJV

*Charm is deceptive,
and beauty does not
last; but a woman
who fears the Lord
will be greatly praised.*

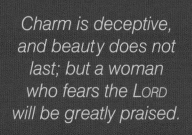

Proverbs 31:30 NLT